First published in Belgium and Holland by Clavis Uitgeverij, Hasselt – Amsterdam, 2013
Copyright © 2013, Clavis Uitgeverij

English translation from the Dutch by Clavis Publishing Inc. New York
Copyright © 2014 for the English language edition: Clavis Publishing Inc. New York

Visit us on the web at www.clavisbooks.com

All About Wild Animals written and illustrated by Mack
Photographs: Shutterstock®
Original title: *Allemaal wilde dieren*
Translated from the Dutch by Clavis Publishing

ISBN 978-1-60537-183-2

This book was printed in April 2014 at Proost, Everdongenlaan 23, 2300 Turnhout, Belgium

First Edition
10 9 8 7 6 5 4 3 2 1

wonderful WORLD

ALL ABOUT WILD ANIMALS

Mack

Clavis

NEW YORK

Funny Animals

PENGUINS

Penguins are very good swimmers. Their webbed feet are good for swimming, but make it hard to walk around on slippery ice. That is why penguins walk a bit weirdly. Step by step they waddle through the snow with their white chests held high and their little black-and-white wings behind their backs. They look so funny! They move slowly, but eventually they get where they're going.

Penguins might look strange when they walk, but they slide really well! They hop – *hop hop* – onto a small hill, then they fall onto their bellies and slide down the hill – head first – *zoom*!

Which penguin can't walk yet?

SLOTHS

Sloths live in trees. These funny animals hang from tree branches, well hidden between the leaves. No one bothers them while they are doing… nothing. Sloths are really lazy. They don't do anything all day but dangle and sleep. Of course they also eat. But sometimes before they get to a yummy leaf, they go back to sleep. Such lazybones!

Sloths do everything hanging from the tree. They hang when they're eating and they hang when they're asleep. They hold onto the branch with strong paws and never let go. That's why sloths never fall out of the trees.

Which tree did the sloth eat?

ZEBRAS

Zebras look like horses wearing pajamas – striped pajamas! Their noses and their tails are black, but the rest of their bodies is covered with black and white stripes. Do you see the white and black stripes on their heads, their necks, their backs, their bellies, their buttocks and their paws? Even their manes are striped. Isn't that pretty?

Zebras can kick really hard
with their hind legs. They're like
soccer players that way.
Except they don't kick forward,
they kick backwards. So be careful!

A zebra's fur is always black-and-white. Do you see the real zebra?

RHINOCEROS

Rhinos have thick skin with lots of folds. The thick skin protects them against the claws and teeth of lions and tigers. With the curved horn on their heads rhinos can protect themselves against dangerous animals. Some rhinos even have two horns – a big one and a smaller one.

Rhinos can't see very well. If they're not careful they bump into trees. They could probably use glasses! Rhinos sometimes get help from friendly birds who chirp really loudly when there is danger.

Which bird is warning the rhino about the snake?

SKUNKS

Skunks have soft hair, small heads, and giant tails. They can't see very well, but they have an excellent sense of smell and are always following their noses. Skunks look very sweet and you might want to pet them. But you'd better not, because skunks don't like to be petted. And to chase you away they spray a really bad scent. It's so bad you'll run away as fast as you can.

Skunks warn people
and animals before
they start to spray.
They shake their funny
tails, stand on their
forepaws and point
the back of their tails
at you. When they
do that, you'd better
start running!

Which skunk do you think is about to spray?

FLAMINGOS

Flamingos love pink. Look at their beautiful pink feathers! Not all flamingos are pink though. Some are grey and others are white. They all have crooked beaks and yellow eyes. Flamingos are crazy about water and they spend all day in it. When they stand still flamingos often stand on one leg. They even sleep on one leg!

Flamingos eat upside down. They bend their necks and use their beaks to scoop small fish from the water. Their favorite meal is little pink shrimp. That is why flamingos are so pretty and pink themselves!

Which flamingos are standing on one leg?

DROMEDARIES

Dromedaries and camels look very much alike. They both live in the hot desert. In the desert the sun shines all day long and it almost never rains. Still, dromedaries and camels walk around cheerfully in the hot sand. Do they get hungry or thirsty? They don't, because they store water and food in those funny humps on their backs! Isn't that smart?

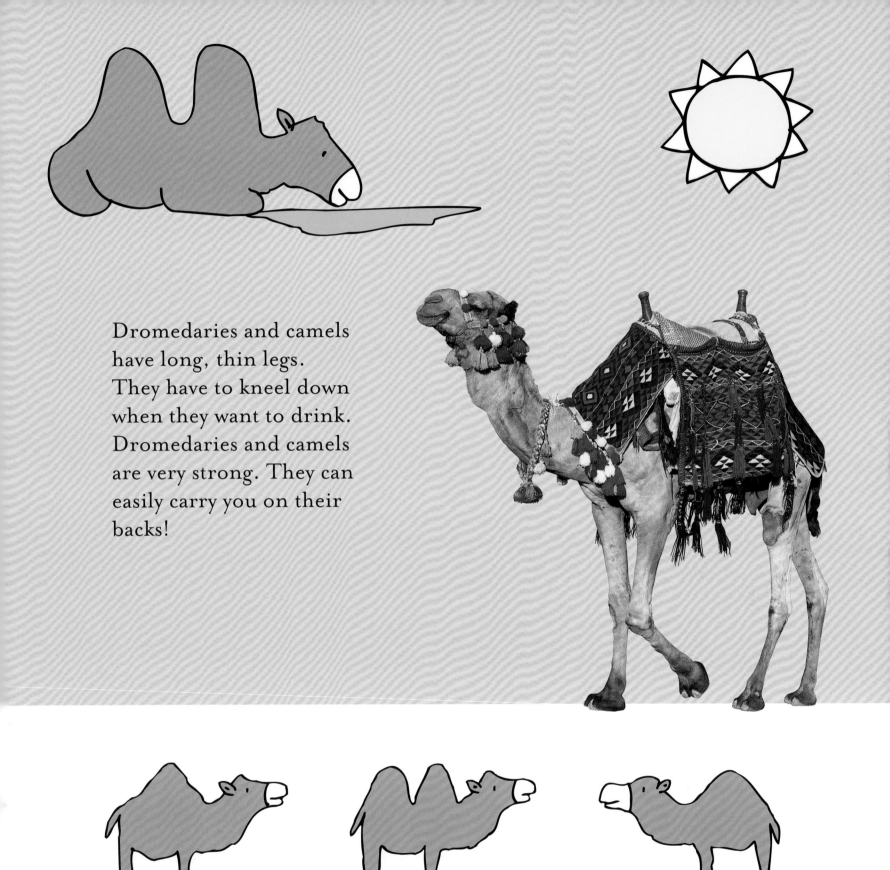

Dromedaries and camels have long, thin legs. They have to kneel down when they want to drink. Dromedaries and camels are very strong. They can easily carry you on their backs!

A camel has two humps and a dromedary has only one. Do you see the camel?

TOUCANS

Toucans are very special birds. They have a beak and wings, just like all birds. But the toucan's beak is much bigger than those of other birds. It's a whopper! The toucan's beak is not only big, it is also beautiful and brightly colored. Yellow, green, blue, black, red, purple, orange – it's as if the toucan wants to say: here I am!

The beaks of toucans might be huge, but they're not very heavy. They're light enough for the birds to be able to fly, and the birds can easily move their heads around – in spite of the size of their beaks!

Can you find the toucan?

Cute Animals

KOALAS

Koalas almost never touch the ground, they live their whole lives high up in the trees. Although they're excellent climbers, they usually just lie lazily on a branch and sleep almost all day long. With their long flat noses, their bright eyes, and their fluffy ears, koalas look really cute.

Koalas only eat leaves from eucalyptus trees, and find all their food in the trees. They search until they find their favorite food. Yummy, delicious!

One koala is still awake. Can you see which one?

DOLPHINS

Dolphins live in the sea. They swim in groups and take good care of each other. Dolphins talk to each other by making funny little sounds. It seems as if they are laughing. Dolphins have to come up for air every now and then. They breathe through small holes in their heads. Sometimes they jump out of the water and come down in an arc. Wow!

Dolphins love playing games and doing tricks. Sometimes they swim alongside a boat and put on a show for the people in the boat. They jump high in the air, spin and stand up on their tails!

Which dolphin is still in the water?

PANDAS

Pandas live in China. With their black-and-white coats they are easy to spot between the juicy, green bamboo stalks. But if you take a trip to China you probably won't run into a panda because there aren't many pandas left. If you do happen to see a panda, he's sure to be sitting on his bottom with a stalk of bamboo in his mouth. Pandas love bamboo.

Pandas love playing games. They fool around and roll on the ground and over each other. Mommy pandas love to play and cuddle with their panda kids.

Which pandas are looking at each other?

ELEPHANTS

Elephants have big ears and long trunks. They are incredibly big and heavy, and are very strong. Elephants are also very sweet. They take good care of their little ones and give each other kisses with their trunks. Isn't that sweet? Elephants make funny noises with their long trunks – they sound like trumpets! It's usually very hot where elephants live. To cool down they flap their ears.

Elephants can do a lot of things with their trunks. They pull grass up from the ground and pick food from the trees. Elephants also use their trunks to wash themselves. They suck water from the river and then...*Splash*! What a lovely shower!

Which elephants have big behinds and which have skinny ones?

ORANGUTANS

Orangutans have very long arms. The cute apes use them to climb the trees. They swing from one tree to the other using their arms and legs. First they grab a branch with one hand – *swing* – and then with the other hand. They do the same with their feet. That's how orangutans move through the jungle.

Orangutans love fruit.
They eat small berries,
juicy mangos and, of course,
bananas. Yummy! All apes
love bananas! Orangutans
also love nuts. They can
crack them with their teeth!

Which orangutan is getting wet?

MEERKATS

Meerkats sleep in burrows deep under the desert sand. These little animals are unbelievably good diggers, and they make long passages and small holes under the ground. In those underground villages they live cozily together. The cute meerkats are afraid to go outside. First one sticks his little head above the sand, then another one, and eventually they all come out.

Birds of prey think meerkats are delicious. That's why there are always a few meerkats on the lookout. They stand on their hind legs and can see very far. "Careful, there is a bird," they call. "Run!"

Which meerkat doesn't see the bird coming?

POLAR BEARS

Polar bears live in the Arctic. It's always very cold over there. So cold that it's icy and snowy all year round. Because of their warm white coats polar bears don't feel the cold. They love playing in the snow. Standing on two paws or rolling around on the ground, polar bears are crazy about snow games!

Polar bears can jump
from ice floe to ice floe.
And when they want to eat,
they make a hole in the ice
and wait for a nice fish
to come out. *Snap*!

There are all sorts of bears. Do you recognize the polar bear?

SEALS

Seals love to be in the water. They can swim fast and very well, and they love doing tricks. They jump and dive and sometimes it even looks like they're waving their flippers. Seals also leave the water every now and again. They crawl on their bellies and drag themselves forward over the ground with their flippers. Usually they're looking for a nice place on dry land where they can sleep in the sun.

Seals have short flippers –
that's why they can't sit up
straight. Sea lions look
a lot like seals, but they
have bigger flippers –
which is why they can
sit up nicely. Isn't that
amazing?

A walrus is a seal with teeth. Do you see the walrus?

DANGEROUS ANIMALS

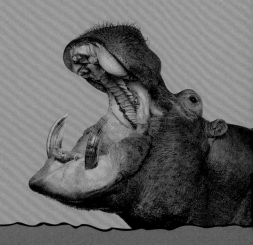

GORILLAS

Gorillas are the biggest apes in the jungle. They are incredibly strong and look very dangerous. All animals in the jungle avoid them, but gorillas are actually very shy. They walk around showing their muscles and looking tough, but they wouldn't hurt a fly. Gorillas don't like eating animals, they prefer green leaves and juicy fruit. *Yummy*, tough gorillas think *green leaves are the most delicious thing in the world!*

Male gorillas like to show that they are the boss by acting big and strong. When other animals want to fight, gorillas beat their chests and roar. They hope it will scare off the other animals, so they won't have to fight.

Male gorillas are also called silverbacks. Do you see the real one?

SHARKS

Sharks have big fins on their backs. All fish swim the other way as fast as they can when they see that shark fin. Sharks are the hunters of the sea. They can swim awfully fast, have good noses, and razor-sharp teeth! Sharks eat little fish in one bite. *Snap*! Sometimes, a shark will accidentally go after a human swimmer. That's only because the shark mistakes the human for a delicious seal.

Sharks' teeth are sharp and very strong. They can even bite through a turtle's shell! When they bite something hard, a few teeth can fall out of the shark's mouth. But they just grow back, so the shark can hunt again.

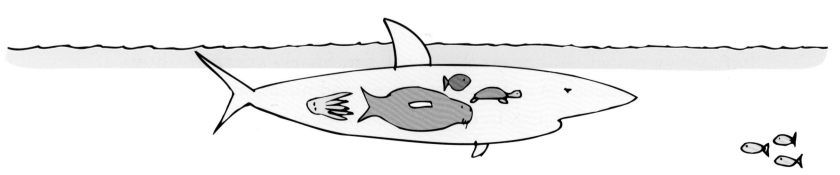

Which animals does this shark have in his belly?

LIONS

Lions can roar really loud. *Rrrrooooar!* They look very dangerous with their strong paws, their sharp claws and their big teeth. Male lions have long manes around their heads, which make them look bigger and stronger. The female lions – called lionesses – do not. Because they look so royal, so noble and strong, lions are called "King of the jungle".

Usually the lionesses do
the hunting for the group.
When the lionesses catch
something, lions are the
first ones there to get
the best piece of meat.
Mommy lions carry their
babies in their mouths.
They are very careful not
to hurt the baby with their
sharp teeth!

Do you recognize daddy, mommy and baby lion?

TIGERS

Tigers have orange and white fur and black stripes. The orange color catches the eye in the jungle, but tigers are very good at playing hide-and-seek. They crawl away behind a bush and then patiently wait for an animal to come by. With one jump the tiger catches the animal. Those dangerous tigers can jump very far and very high.

Tigers love water and often take baths. That's how they keep their striped fur clean. They're very good swimmers and can easily cross big rivers. Well done!

Which tiger is a fake one? Why?

HIPPOPOTAMUSES

Hippopotamuses are very big and heavy. They don't like the heat and prefer to float in the cool water all day. Sometimes you can only see the hippo's eyes and ears peeping out of the water. Hippos have big mouths with strong teeth. They open their mouths wide to yawn, but sometimes also to fight. Hippos might look sweet and slow, but they are dangerous creatures!

Hippos don't have
hair on their backs
to protect them
against the sun.
That's why they love
to take mud baths!

Which baby hippo doesn't look happy?

KOMODO DRAGONS

Komodo dragons are the biggest lizards in the world. They can be found on just a few tropical islands. If you ever happen to go to those islands, you'd better look out. Komodo dragons are dangerous meat-eaters and they eat just about anything – even animals that are bigger than the komodo dragons themselves. They eat humans too! That is why komodo dragons are also called monsters. *Ugh*.

Komodo dragons can do something really special. They can smell with their tongues! Their split tongues hang out of their mouths all the time. With their tongues komodo dragons can smell if you're a yummy bite or not.

The komodo dragon is a lizard. Do you see two other lizards?

CROCODILES

Crocodiles are crazy about water. They are almost exactly the same green and brown color as the jungles and rivers around them, so you have to look carefully to find them. Even when they are walking between plants or sunbathing on the bank you can hardly see them. But when crocodiles open their jaws you can spot them in a second. Their enormous crocodile mouths are filled with sharp teeth. Very dangerous!

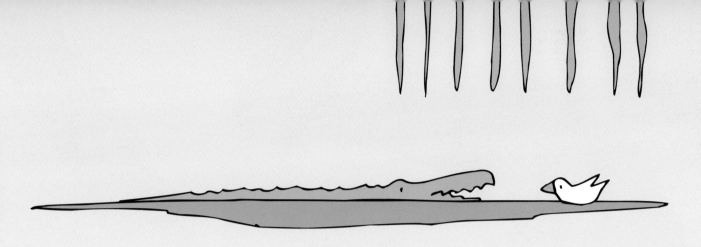

Crocodiles can lie still in the water
for hours. But when they spot a yummy
little bird or a fish they move quickly and
suddenly. Mother crocodiles also pick up
their babies with their jaws. They do it
very carefully of course!

Which animal has the biggest mouth?

LEOPARDS

Leopards are very dangerous. They might look like big cats, but be careful. You'd better not pet leopards, because their claws and teeth are as strong as those of a lion! Leopards love climbing and are very good at it. When a leopard catches a tasty animal with his dangerous teeth, he sometimes takes it up into a tree. Then he lies on a branch to eat.

Black leopards
are called black
panthers. They hunt
in the dark. You can
hardly see them
because of their
beautiful black fur.
Their eyes are the
only things shining
in the moonlight.

Do you see the real black panther?

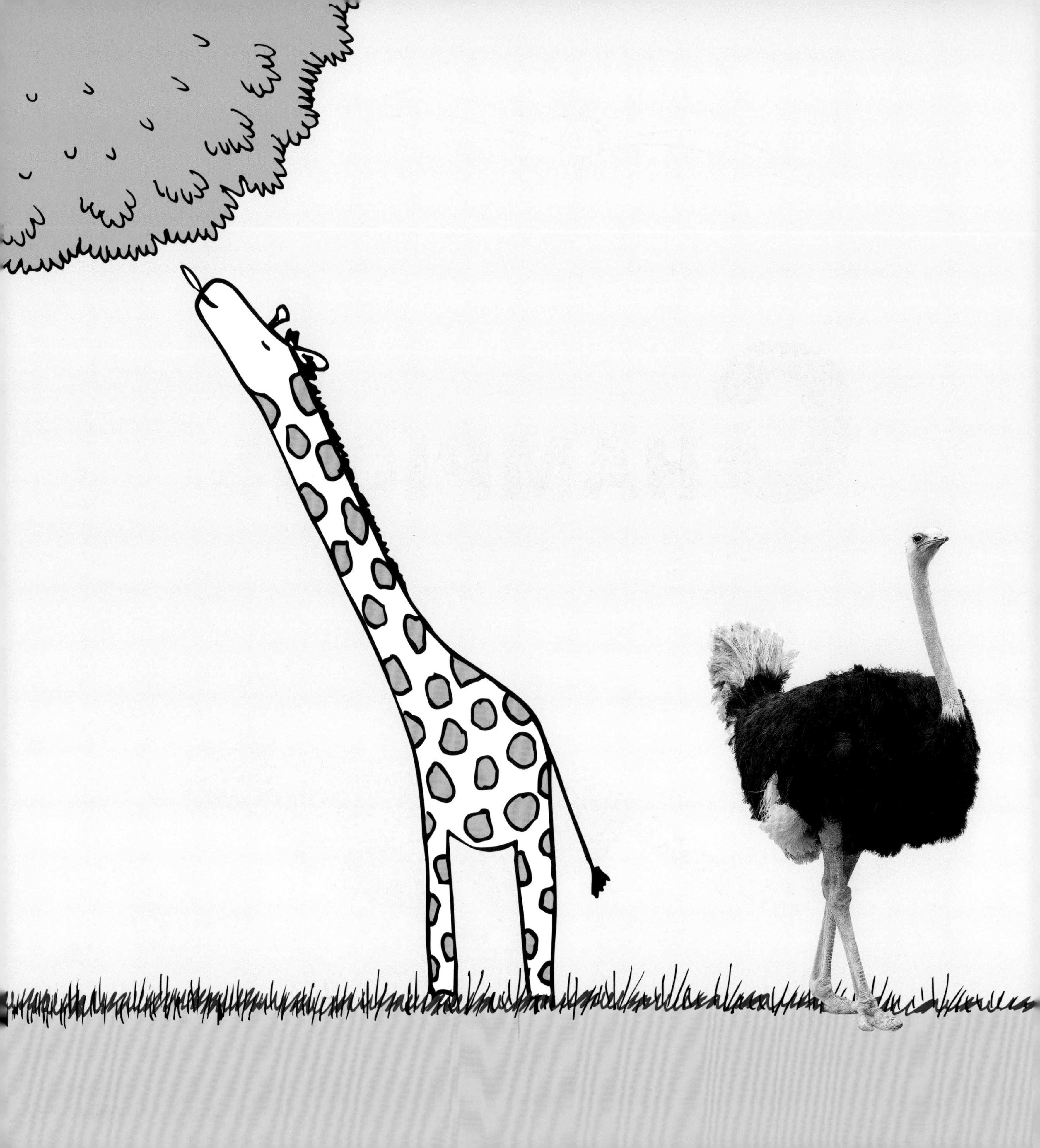

CHAMPIONS

CHEETAHS

Cheetahs are fast runners. They are *very* fast runners. When cheetahs see a yummy bite they immediately duck into the tall grass. They quietly steal closer and closer until they are right behind the other animal. And then cheetahs run as swiftly as arrows. *Zoom!* Within two strides cheetahs can run faster than a horse. And then they go even faster. Almost as fast as a car!

Cheetahs can run this fast because they can stretch all the way. They shoot through the brown grass like rubber bands. Then you can't count all the spots on their backs. That's how fast they run!

Which cheetah has the most spots?

ALBATROSSES

Albatrosses can fly very far. They live in groups on islands where they build their nests and lay their eggs. When the baby albatrosses are born, mommy or daddy goes to look for food very far away. Sometimes they even go to the other end of the sea. Albatrosses can fly a very long way in order to catch a good fish. Days later they return with a fish they caught in a different country. Isn't that amazing?

Albatrosses need a long run before they can take off into the sky. But when they finally spread their big wings, they can float like a kite in the air for a very long while without moving their wings. Albatrosses are floating champions.

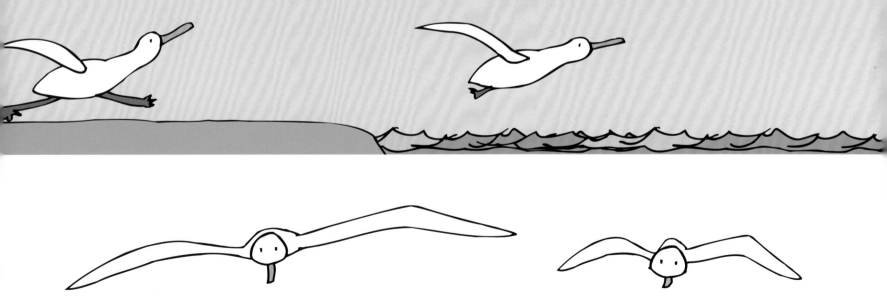

Albatrosses have very big wings. Do you see the real albatross?

KANGAROOS

Kangaroos have four paws: two short forepaws and two big, powerful hind legs. They can't walk, they can only jump. And they jump very high and very far. When there's a bush or a fallen tree in their way they don't have to take a run-up, they simply jump over them. *Hop hop!*

Mommy kangaroos have
a pouch on their bellies.
Those warm pockets are
the perfect place for the
baby kangaroos to sit.
Until little kangaroos
can jump all by themselves,
their mothers carry them.
Thank you, mommy
kangaroo!

Kangaroos don't fall over because they have long tails to balance them.
Which tail looks weird?

BROWN BEARS

Brown bears love sleeping. They fall asleep anytime and anywhere –
in the forest, in the grass, or lazily against a tree trunk. Brown bears have
the best time when they just close their eyes and snore. In the winter when
it's cold out, bears sleep for a very long time. Not for just one day, or one
night or even one week, but for the whole winter!

When bears are awake,
they often get itchy.
They can't reach their
own backs with their
paws, so they look for
a tree to rub against.
Hmm, that feels good.
Now it's time for a nap!
Zzzz.

What do you think is the brown bear's favorite food?

OSTRICHES

Ostriches are birds that can't fly. They are far too big and far too heavy to go up in the air. That's why they prefer to walk. And they are very good walkers too. Have you ever taken a close look at the ostriches' feet? They have just two toes on each foot. They can run really fast with those feet though – faster than zebras and lions, and even faster than wild dogs. They are the running champions of the birds.

Mommy ostriches lay
big eggs and ostrich
chicks are very big when
they are born. When
they leave the egg they
are already as big as
a fully-grown chicken!

Which ostrich is the better dancer?

GIRAFFES

Giraffes are so tall, they tower above everything else. They are taller than rhinoceroses, taller than elephants, even taller than some trees. Because their necks are so long, giraffes can easily eat the leaves from the tops of trees. That's where the best leaves are – at the very top. Giraffes stick their long necks all the way out, and with their very long tongues they pick the leaves no other animal can reach. Yummy, that's delicious!

When giraffes want to drink they have to bend their necks very far down. Eating is easier. Not only because of their long necks, but also because of those long legs.

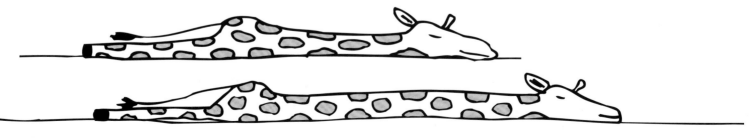

Which giraffe has the longest neck?

MOUNTAIN GOATS

Mountain goats live in the mountains. Not just at the bottom or halfway up the mountain, but in the part of the mountain that's so high no trees can grow. That's where mountain goats live between the rocks. They can easily climb any rock with their strong hooves. Once they are all the way up, mountain goats look around to see if there are more mountains around. If there are, they can keep climbing.

Mountain goats eat grass
and bushes. They'll do anything
to find a nice piece of grass.
Sometimes they stretch,
but mostly they just climb.
Mountain goats are climbing
champions!

Which mountain goats are very good at climbing and which ones still have to learn?

WHALES

Whales are the biggest animals in the world. They are even bigger than elephants. If you put a family of elephants in a row: daddy elephant, mommy elephant, aunt elephant, granny elephant and all the kid elephants, then together they would be as big as one whale. To grow so incredibly big whales eat a lot of small fish. Their mouths are big enough to park a bus inside, so a whole lot of tiny fish fit in there.

Sperm whales are whales with flat noses. Sperm whales can dive really deep to look for the giant squids they love to eat. Black whales with white patches are called orcas. They can jump out of the water in a graceful arc.

On the whale's head there is a hole out of which water spurts. Do you see it?